Better Homes and Gardens®

# SHRUBS

## The Gardener's Collection

Better Homes and Gardens® Books

Des Moines

*All of us at Meredith® Books are dedicated to providing you
with the information and ideas you need to garden success-
fully. We guarantee your satisfaction with this book for as
long as you own it. If you have any questions, comments, or
suggestions,*
*please write to us at:*

MEREDITH® BOOKS, Garden Books
Editorial Department, RW 240
1716 Locust St.
Des Moines, IA  50309-3023

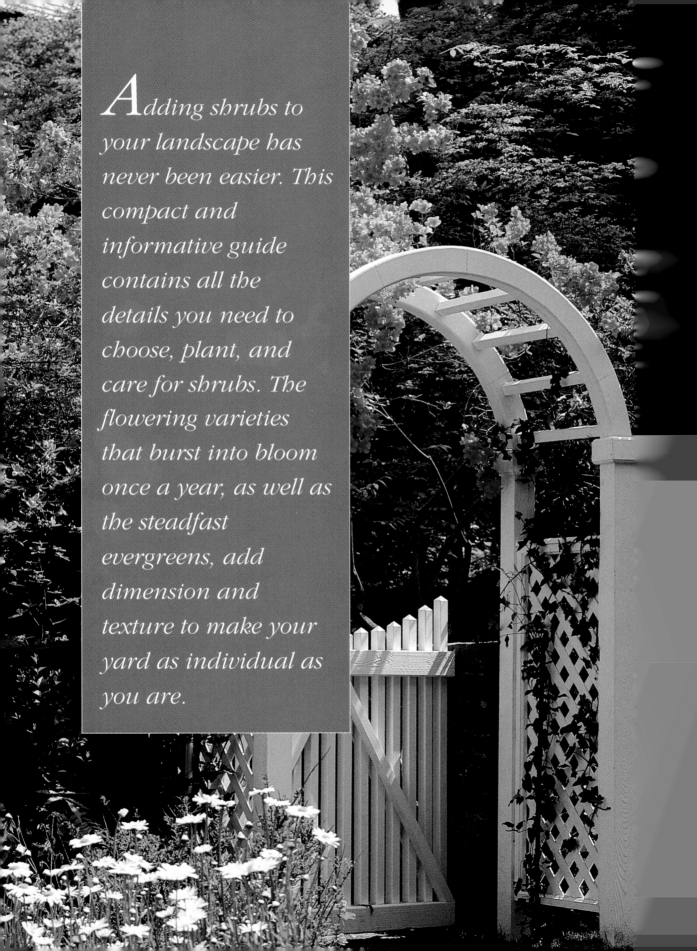

*Adding shrubs to your landscape has never been easier. This compact and informative guide contains all the details you need to choose, plant, and care for shrubs. The flowering varieties that burst into bloom once a year, as well as the steadfast evergreens, add dimension and texture to make your yard as individual as you are.*

# CONTENTS

# DIRECTORY OF SHRUBS 32

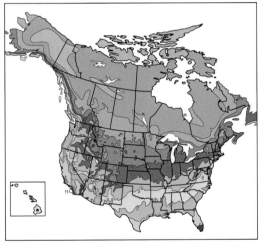

# ZONE MAP 62

# INDEX 64

## Choosing Shrubs

*A*vailable in staggering variety and numbers, shrubs are often the backbone of a good landscape design. Visually diverse, flowering shrubs, narrow-leaved evergreens, and broad-leaved evergreens may be ground hugging or tall. Used as privacy screens, foundation plants, or eye-catching specimens, shrubs solve myriad gardening problems.

# Shrub Types and Uses

**Versatile** and valuable in lanscapes, shrubs can dress up, cover up, or accent a home's features. Whether selected as the finishing touch to a landscape plan or as the first effort to soften the look of new construction, shrubs have earned a rightful place as a quick and easy answer to many landscaping problems: quick, because most shrubs grow rapidly, promising good bloom and spreading in the first season after planting; easy, because many shrubs are hardy and can withstand minimal care and even drought.

**Three basic types** are available: deciduous flowering shrubs, broad-leaved evergreens, and narrow-leaved evergreens.

**What to Plant** For an approach to landscape design that will mean less work for you, consider the natural shapes of shrubs available in your part of the country.

Deciduous shrubs have four typical shapes: arching branches, erect, rounded, and spreading. Evergreens, on the other hand, have five basic growth patterns: low and trailing, medium spreading, horizontal spreading, round compact, and upright.

**For informal borders,** use rounded forms. Most mature plants in this group will spread up to 6 feet, so give them plenty of room.

Vertical lines characterize erect or upright forms, making them perfect accents. They're good as narrow hedges but need pruning.

With graceful, fountainlike silhouettes, arching shrubs add a restful touch to the garden. Use them for shrub borders or as specimen plants.

Large spreading types provide horizontal lines, accenting a home's architecture; use them as foreground plants.

*Japanese kerria is one of the few shrubs to flower well in the shade.*

*Almost carefree, honeysuckle can grow to 8 feet tall if left unpruned.*

# Where to Plant Shrubs

## Shapely Shrubs

### ARCHING BRANCHES
Beautybush
Butterfly bush
Daphne, lilac
Deutzia, slender
Forsythia
Spirea

### ERECT
Cranberry, highbush
Dogwood, red-osier
Hibiscus
Lilac, common
Mock orange, lemoine

### ROUNDED
Hydrangea
Kerria
Lilac, Persian
Quince, flowering
Weigela
Witch hazel

### SPREADING
Cotoneaster, spreading
Crab apple, sargent
Ninebark, dwarf
Quince, Japanese
Sumac, staghorn
Viburnum, fragrant

**Shrubs can accent** the best architectural features of a home or hide bare, boring spots such as foundation walls. Shrubs also can help blend a house with its surroundings. Try to plant shrubs where strong vertical architectural lines meet the ground.

**At the front of a house,** use a strong corner grouping. To emphasize an entrance, use tall accent plantings at either side of the doorway. Evergreens with upright, rounded, or pointed shapes are effective. For a special touch, add an accent plant such as a flowering clematis. Place lower-growing plants under windows. Use short hedges or dwarf shrubs in a front border to unify a house and site and as a textured background for bedding flowers.

**Along the side** of a house keep plantings simple. For best effect, group three or more of the same kind of shrub together. If your home has a high foundation, use large shrubs at the corners, adding vines on one as an accent.

*A compact, hardy hibiscus looks best near an entryway.*

*An interplay of spring colors accents an approach to the house.*

# Spring Beauties

Like Cinderella dressed for the ball, many useful shrubs are transformed each spring into ravishing beauties arrayed colorfully in blossoms that delight the senses.

After a bleak winter, flowering shrubs cheerfully reward a bit of pruning and some fertilizing with lovely foliage and otherwise carefree maintenance.

In selecting flowering varieties, give some thought to their blooming sequence, as well as to the color and size of blossoms.

Plan your garden with an eye to the hues and tints of those blooms. Some gardeners keep to a single color—all orange, red, white, or lavender, for example. Others blend shades within a range—yellow with orange and orange with red, perhaps.

You'll be happiest massing several of the same kind of shrub and blossom color. One of everything may give a polka-dot effect, causing the eye to jump from one color to another.

## Gardener's Tip

Shrubs with flowers that bloom on new wood (this year's growth) should be pruned in early spring while plants are still dormant. Shape up shrubs that bloom on old wood (last year's growth) after the flowers fade.

*A specimen (or single) plant makes a spectacular statement. The giant, softball-size blooms of snowball viburnum weigh down branches like the beautiful burden of a heavy spring snow. Scaled-down hybrids of old-fashioned weigela squeeze more easily into today's smaller yards.*

# Private Views

A private yard, like a tranquil island, has irresistible allure. And you can create your own outdoor sanctum without a chain-link, wood, or stone fence. Shrubbery screens can be more effective than any of these at blocking noise, wind, sun, and visual intrusion—and be more eye-catching, too.

**Form Follows Function** Define your objective before selecting shrubs for your screen. Is your goal to divide or define an area? Create an impenetrable screen? Plant evergreens for year-round protection and privacy; use flowering deciduous shrubs to create a temporary decorative and friendly screen.

Tall, hedgelike shrubs, whether evergreen or dense deciduous varieties, create excellent background plantings. These upright forms also require less horizontal space in the garden.

Flowering shrubs make colorful accents in a garden each spring and summer, and can be intermingled with evergreens or massed together in a border for a hedgelike effect.

**Creating Your Privacy Screen** Whether used to divide one section of a garden from another or to separate properties, living privacy screens offer the chance for beautiful combinations of texture, color, and size.

Start at the back with taller shrubs. Plants growing 7 feet high make good choices for most screens. They will undoubtedly be much smaller when you buy them, so leave space between them when planting so they'll have room to grow to maturity.

**Working with Colors** For best results with flowering screens, follow the basic principles of color theory. Deeply colored flowers recede when contrasted with dark foliage; when set against a light yellow-green background, they stand out. In shady areas, light-toned flowers look best. Brilliant flowers are striking in a sunny spot next to a pale or white-toned wall.

*Tall ficus shrubs form a high screen with a stately presence.*

Mix hot red or scarlet with pink or pastels for a lively color combination. Strong yellow and pink hues are jarring, but a blend of yellow and yellow-orange hues works well. Red is at its best with white, and yellow-pink hues shine against white backdrops.

**Maintenance** Before you plant for privacy think about how much time you want to spend maintaining it. The more formal the choice, the more pruning and clipping may be needed. Maybe you're willing to prune those lilacs or forsythias once a year in exchange for the enjoyment of the flowers. If not, shop in the evergreen department.

# Hedge Basics

Like a decorative wall, a hedge marks a boundary, dividing the yard while giving it an orderly pattern, whether prim or playful. Hedges may be real barriers or act as graceful guardians of paths and flower beds.

**Height Options** Low, high, or between, the height of a hedge depends on its purpose, the kind of shrub selected, and how often you trim it. As always with shrubs, choosing the best type for the soil, the site, and the landscape design is essential.

Low hedges, 1 to 3 feet tall, must be slow growing and neat, and must tolerate regular pruning. If you want to keep a hedge less than 2 feet tall, shearing is a must. To keep plants within bounds, begin training them the first year.

Medium hedges, 3 to 5 feet tall, include azaleas, many types of yews, and roses. Use a medium-tall hedge to screen unsightly areas in the yard, such as storage of trash containers. For an informal look, clip a hedge annually or semiannually to keep plants compact.

A tall hedge, 5 feet or more, is an elegant background planting. For centuries, close-clipped hedges of boxwood, yew, cypress, and holly have bordered the beds and boundaries of formal gardens.

**Positioning the Hedge** Placing shrubs is a little like putting together a jigsaw puzzle. What you see in the nursery may only be a youngster, perhaps a fifth of its mature size; better to imagine 0the shrub's appearance at maturity.

■ For an informal hedge, plant shrubs in two staggered rows to give a wider base and fuller growth for better screening.

■ For a formal hedge, dig a trench so shrubs can be planted single file.

■ Spacing varies with species but a general rule is to plant shrubs 12 inches apart if the hedge is to be trimmed 2 feet tall. For a 4-foot tall hedge, space 18 inches apart; 4 feet apart for a 6- to 8-foot screen.

*Disciplined arborvitae can be pruned to any height and makes an excellent all-green screen. Less formal is bridal wreath spirea, which produces tiny white spring flowers.*

# Special-Interest Shrubs

## QUICK-GROWING SCREENS

Beautybush
Elaeagnus
Euonymus
Forsythia
Honeysuckle
Mock orange
Privet
Viburnum:
    arrowwood
    nannyberry
    siebold

## SPRING-FLOWERING SHRUBS

Andromeda
Azalea, Korean
Barberry
Bayberry
Cinquefoil
Forsythia
Fruit, dwarf
Honeysuckle
Kerria
Lilac
Pussy willow
Rhododendron
Spirea
Viburnum
Witch hazel

## SUMMER-FLOWERING SHRUBS

Arrowwood
Azalea, flame
Butterfly bush
Crape myrtle
Hydrangea, peegee
Leucothoe
Mock orange
Mountain laurel
Privet
Rose-of-sharon
Spirea
    'Anthony Waterer'
Stewartia

## FRAGRANT SHRUBS

Azalea hybrids
Bayberry
Boxwood
Butterfly bush
Clethra
Honeysuckle
Lilac
Privet
Rhododendron hybrids
Rose
Viburnum, Korean spice
Witch hazel

## FRUITING SHRUBS

Almond
Apple
Apricot
Blueberry
Cherry, bush
Cherry, Surinam
Citrus, dwarf
Currant
Gooseberry
Guava, pineapple
Nectarine
Peach
Pear
Plum
Pomegranate
Quince

## FOLIAGE SHRUBS FOR SHADE

Boxwood
Cypress, false
Euonymus
Holly
Leucothoe
Privet
Yew

*The horizontal branching of double-file viburnum is attractive any time of year, but showy white blooms are a big sensation every spring.*

## FLOWERING SHRUBS FOR SHADE

Andromeda
Azalea
Buckeye, bottlebrush
Camellia
Clethra
Fuchsia
Hydrangea
Kerria
Mahonia
Mountain laurel

## Care and Maintenance

*Shrubs are among the easiest plants to care for. Except for pruning, you'll need to spend a minimum amount of time to keep them at their beautiful best. Once you're familiar with the basics of plant life—soil, water, and light—you can nurture your investment in tomorrow.*

# Planting Shrubs

Shrubs solve many landscaping problems, but when making plant choices, carefully consider their needs first. Do they require sun or shade? Wet or dry soil? What are their pruning requirements, and do they need protection in winter? Check the Directory of Shrubs (pages 32–61) for recommendations before digging any holes.

**Shrub Forms** You can buy shrubs from a nursery in three forms: bare root, balled and burlapped, and container grown.

Bare-root shrubs are best planted in winter or early spring. Keep the roots moist until you're ready to plant. Dig a hole somewhat larger than the root area. Plan to set the shrub slightly deeper than it was before. Lay a shovel handle across the hole to help determine proper planting depth.

Mold a loose cone of soil in the bottom of the hole, then set the shrub in the hole and spread its roots over the cone. Backfill the hole halfway, tamping the soil slightly around the roots. Give the plant a good soaking, then fill with remaining soil.

Although more expensive than bare-root plants, balled-and-burlapped shrubs and shrubs grown in containers are available during peak gardening seasons. To plant balled-and-burlapped or container shrubs, dig a hole a foot wider than the root ball and about as deep. Lower the root ball carefully and center it.

If balled, loosen the burlap around the trunk, but you need not remove it. Burlap decays rapidly and will not interfere with root development. If the shrub is wrapped in plastic, or is in an asphalt or cardboard container, cut the wrap or container, then remove it after positioning the root ball in the hole.

If the plant is in a metal container, ask the nursery to cut slits in the container before you take it home. Then remove it and place the plant in the hole. For both balled and container shrubs, backfill the hole as for bare-root shrubs.

**Caring for New Shrubs** To help catch water, form a shallow depression around the trunk of the newly planted shrub. Give the shrub a good soaking after planting. In a few days, water it deeply again.

Trim the plant back to one-fourth of its original height if you plan to keep it sheared, one-half for an informal look. Shear all evergreens to a uniform size and shape. Place mulch all the way around the base, to within an inch or two of the trunk.

## Gardener's Tip

When you dig the planting hole for a shrub, make refilling the hole easier. Put a tarp or piece of plastic next to where you'll dig the hole, then place the soil on it.

# More Planting Basics

**Moving Mature Shrubs** The best time to build a patio, add a much-needed room to the house, or install off-street parking may not be the best time to move a shrub. So what do you do with a shrub growing right in the middle of a construction site?

It can be moved safely and with a minimum of shock in the heat of midsummer. In fact, this is a better time than earlier in the season. A shrub lifted in early summer will have more tender foliage.

A few days before transplanting, use a sharp spade and sink its blade completely into the ground in a circle around the shrub. A small shrub should have a circle with a 12-inch radius (at least 18 inches for larger shrubs). Some of the roots will be cut in the process, so also trim off the soft, tender tips of all branches.

**As a protective step,** you may want to spray the shrub with an antidesiccant, available at many garden centers. (It is relatively expensive, so you may want to eliminate this step.) Allow the spray to dry before digging the shrub. The thin film will hold moisture in the plant and help prevent wilting and loss of roots.

Shape roots and surrounding soil into a ball by undercutting lower roots. When the ball is free and can be rocked to one side, use a wide strip of burlap to wind around the ball and hold the soil during moving. Use nails to hold the burlap to the soil. Fasten the top with twine.

The balled-and-burlapped shrub—even a small one—is heavy, so you'll need help to get the plant out of the hole. If the shrub is large, slide a board under the ball and weight the free end to raise the plant.

Move the shrub to a shady spot protected from the wind. Spray the burlap with water and cover it with a plastic sheet until planting.

Planting the mature shrub is nearly the same as planting other balled-and-burlapped shrubs, a process described on page 22. Let the burlap remain on the root ball after it's placed in the hole, but remove the twine fastening. Fill the hole with soil and water as before.

Euonymus, viburnum, mock orange, and privet shrubs all transplant well in the summer. Evergreens cannot be moved safely until the new spring growth has matured.

**Caring for Transplanted Shrubs**
For the next two weeks, cool the plant daily during hot weather with a light mist from a hose. Avoid overwatering; after two weeks, watering once a week is enough for a transplanted shrub. Do not water in the hot sun.

## Gardener's Tip

Plastic sheeting can help keepweeds under control. When planting a formal hedge, lay plastic along the string line. Cut holes as needed and insert plants.

**Planting a Formal Hedge** Plan to set plants at least half their mature width from property lines. Lay a string line as a guide. For the cleanest edge, strip the sod. Dig a trench or large hole as deep as the root system. Prepare the soil well, adding humus generously.

Set the shrub at the same level as at the nursery. Adjust each plant to keep it vertical and in line. Spacing varies with shrub type.

**Caring for a Young Hedge** A young hedge will need ample watering its first summer. Prune the sides of a new hedge frequently to help spur sprouting and denser branching. Let the top grow to the desired height, then trim along the sides as needed. Shear the hedge so it tapers toward the top to allow plenty of light to reach the sides.

# Nurturing Tips

Every gardener wishes for large and healthy plants. Blue-ribbon gardening depends on a few techniques. Here's a quick review of the basics.

**Types of Soil** Soil consists of three types of particles: sand (the largest); clay (the smallest); and silt (which varies). The ideal soil is loam, which has the right balance of sand, clay, and silt.

Sandy soils dry out quickly and leach fertilizer rapidly but drain well. Clay soils are heavy, hold excessive water, and have poor aeration, yet hold on to fertilizer well. Soil that is heavy with clay will stick to your shovel.

**Improving Soil** You'll rarely find exactly the right soil in your garden; improve it with organic matter such as peat moss, leaf mold, manure, or compost. Work in enough organic matter to make it 25 percent of your finished soil. Dig, spade, or power till the soil to a depth of at least 12 inches but no more than 24. Break large chunks into smaller particles.

Use a tester kit or have the soil tested for you to determine its pH (whether soil is alkaline, neutral, or acid). Add ground dolomitic limestone to raise the pH; add sulfur to lower it.

**Water** Apply an inch of water per watering and don't water again until the surface dries. Avoid watering on windy or very hot days to reduce evaporation. One heavy, deep watering is better than several shallow ones.

Water shrubs weekly when weather is hot or dry. Water in the morning if you use sprinklers. Drip irrigation tends to use less water and produce better growth. Two to 3 inches of mulch helps conserve moisture in soil and cuts down the amount of water needed. Do not lay mulch all the way to the shrub's stems; direct contact may cause rot. Learn about water-conservation methods to protect resources.

**Fertilizer** Think of fertilizer as nutrition for your plants. Organic fertilizers come from animal and plant wastes such as blood meal, manure, and cottonseed meal. Synthetic organics include urea, ureaformaldehyde, and IBDU. Inorganic fertilizers are chemicals such as potassium, ammonium nitrates and ammonium phosphates. Each type has good and bad qualities; get more information and decide for yourself which you prefer.

Fertilize shrubs when growth is at its peak or when the plant is producing flowers or fruits. Late fall and early spring are other recommended times. Use a fertilizer rich in phosphorus for flowering shrubs. Feed nonflowering shrubs when you feed the lawn, with the same fertilizer. Apply fertilizer evenly to the soil as far as the branches reach to cover the entire root zone.

**Insects and diseases** may affect your shrubs. For insurance against insects, use a dormant oil spray on flowering shrubs in early spring before buds break. Sprays also can control scales, aphids, and mites on many evergreen and deciduous plants.

*Soil high in clay (top) forms a tight, sticky mass if squeezed when wet. Sandy soil (center) feels grainy and crumbles when wet. Loam (bottom) molds into a loose mound when squeezed lightly. Squeezed harder, it crumbles.*

# Pruning Primer

Most deciduous shrubs can survive and some may even thrive if never pruned. To control size, improve shape, or remove dead wood, however, pruning is necessary and desirable. Pruning also encourages flowering and discourages disease and insect infestations.

**Timing** For best results, prune winter-hardy deciduous shrubs in winter or early spring, shaping plants before new leaves and flowers appear. Early pruning promotes healing and gives you a bare-branch framework to study.

**How to Prune** The first step when pruning either deciduous or evergreen shrubs is to remove dead wood, broken branches, and weak, spindly twigs. This will help ensure a plant's good health. It might even be enough to please the eye. Prune further only to improve the shrub's shape, using one of the techniques illustrated opposite.

To keep deciduous shrubs sound and shapely, trim the plants back a little bit each year. Prune spring- flowering shrubs, too, when blossoms begin to fade.

For a light heading back, cut one-fourth of the top growth over the crown and sides from any type of shrub. This stimulates side branching and more compact growth. A shrub with a lot of twiggy branches benefits from a hard heading back, or heavy pruning, deep into the crown. To keep the plant well groomed, remove one-fourth of its branches each year, cutting back half their length. Some shrubs, such as hydrangea or red-osier dogwood, demand severe heading back each year to be at peak performance. For severe heading back, cut all the way to the ground.

To rejuvenate an old deciduous shrub, each year for three years cut out about one-third of the oldest canes flush with the base of the shrub. By the third year, your plant will be a more productive specimen with full new growth.

Shrubs pruned heavily each year will need a little extra mulching and fertilizing.

# Pruning Techniques

**To reduce size,** increase bloom, and control shape of a mature plant, remove some of its branch tips Cut directly above a strong bud.

**To increase flower size,** trim all branches back. This stimulates production of a few strong stems and fewer but large, flowers.

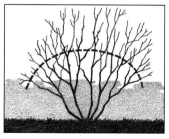

**To rejuvenate an old, bushy shrub** with many limbs, cut out one-third of the older branches at the soil line each year.

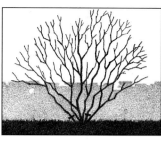

**To remove suckers,** carefully dig away soil and cut them off at the root. Remove suckers unless new growth is needed to rejuvenate plant.

**To make a plant airier and less dense,** thin it by trimming a few limbs back to the ground or main branch.

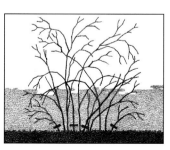

**To keep growth dense,** clip shoots to stimulate limbs to produce more growing points. Use a knife or hand pruners.

**To help keep a plant symmetrical and accent its natural form,** cut off new shoots as they appear.

**To keep plants small,** head-back or thin, depending on the final shape you want the plant to have.

# More Shrub Care

**Pruning evergreens** is more methodical and less creative than pruning other shrubs. A cut of the wrong evergreen branch could mean a huge hole in the shrub for years. Once removed, branches are at best partially replaced. Only when plants become injured, scraggly, diseased, or suffer winterkill should you attempt to severely manicure evergreens.

Most conifers fall into two groups: those pruned after new growth starts (fir, pine, spruce, and hemlock) and those pruned before new growth (juniper, arborvitae, and yew). Limit pruning conifers to correcting problems and cutting branch tips for compact shape and symmetry.

Begin when plants are young, then attend to them regularly but lightly. Cut lower branches only if diseased or dead. Evergreens can look top-heavy if trunks are bare at the bottom, and they rarely fill in.

Prune yew and hemlock with hedge shears. Trim only to reinforce the natural contours of the plant.

Spruce and fir form natural pyramidal shapes. Nip off the terminal buds on their branches as soon as they appear to help laterals grow and strengthen weak branches.

Of all the evergreens, pine needs the least pruning. Prune vigorous new growths (called candles) before they harden. Cutting candles on the main branches to half their length forces laterals, encouraging a fuller plant. Juniper produces dense growth in the spring. Prune early, before this new growth appears. Prune lightly, too, using a shingling technique (trim the upper branches of spreading juniper so they don't overhang the lower branches).

## Winter Protection for Shrubs

■ In cold-winter areas, protect marginally hardy deciduous plants with a thick mulch of leaves, evergreen boughs, or wood chips after frost. Remove in spring.

■ Because evergreens retain their foliage, they are vulnerable to drying winter winds. Watering all

*Shrubs used as hedges should be cut back regularly with hedge clippers to keep them in shape. Sharp pruning shears should be used to head-back evergreens.*

evergreen shrubs deeply before the ground freezes will help.

■ To provide further protection, set up a four-sided burlap screen; fill the gap between screen and shrub with leaves or straw.

■ If snow or ice coats branches, remove it to prevent breakage.

# Directory of Shrubs

*Whether you're starting from scratch with a new landscape plan or sprucing up a long-familiar yard, this directory of shrubs can be a helpful partner. For hundreds of flowering shrubs, narrow-leaved evergreens, and broad-leaved conifers you'll find zone information, plus descriptive details, growing conditions, and tips.*

# FLOWERING (DECIDUOUS) SHRUBS

## ARALIA, FIVE-LEAVED
*Acanthopanax sieboldianus*

**Zone:** 5

**Height:** 3–6 feet

**Foliage and Flowers:** Dark green palmate leaves turn yellow in fall. Sharp spires at leaf base.

**Comments:** Tolerant of most light and soil conditions. Use as foliage plants or as hedges. Soot tolerant.

## AZALEA
(See Rhododendron, page 49.)

## BARBERRY
*Berberis sp.*

### Japanese
*B. thunbergi*

**Zone:** 5

**Height:** 5 feet

**Foliage and Flowers:** Half-inch yellow flowers bordered with red hang on the plant in early spring, followed by bright red oval berries in fall. Bright green foliage, but red-leaved varieties exist. Twigs are thorny. Dwarf form grows to 2 feet.

**Comments:** Full sun or partial shade. Tolerant of most soil types. Use in hedges or as specimen plants. Easily sheared; works as barrier planting. Berries are eaten by birds in winter.

## BEAUTYBUSH
*Kolkwitzia amabilis*

**Zone:** 6

**Height:** 15 feet

**Foliage and Flowers:** Half-inch pink or pink and white flowers, followed by unusual brown seedpods that cling until winter. Foliage turns red in fall. Bark peels attractively.

**Comments:** Full sun or partial shade. Moist, well-drained soil. Branches upright and arching. Use as specimen plants; best grown singly. Needs no pruning or special care.

# BROOM
*Cytisus sp.*

## Scotch
*C. scoparius*

**Zone:** 6

**Height:** 10 feet

**Foliage and Flowers:** Pealike flowers in spring. Mixed colors. Dwarf varieties grow to 2 feet.

**Comments:** Well-drained soil. Full sun. Quick growing. Use as specimen plants. Prune after flowering.

## Spike
*C. nigricans*

**Zone:** 5

**Height:** 6 feet

**Foliage and Flowers:** Yellow, pealike flowers on 6- to 12-inch-long spikes in midsummer.

**Comments:** Full sun. Well-drained soil. Quick growing and hardy. Blooms in all situations.

# BUCKEYE

## Dwarf horse chestnut
*Aesculus parviflora*

**Zone:** 5

**Height:** 15 feet

**Foliage and Flowers:** Half-inch white flowers in spike clusters 10 to 15 inches long in midsummer. Dark green palmately arranged leaves. Yellow leaves in the fall.

**Comments:** Full sun. Moist, well-drained soil. Vigorous and attractive. Forms a dense mound twice as wide as tall. Reproduces by underground suckers. Shiny brown, inedible nuts.

# BUTTERFLY BUSH
*Buddleia sp.*

## Fountain
*B. alternifolia*

**Zone:** 6

**Height:** 12 feet

**Foliage and Flowers:** Quarter-inch lilac-colored flowers on long spikes in early summer. Foliage is an attractive gray-green.

**Comments:** Full sun. Well-drained soil. Vigorous and hardy. Use as a specimen plant in large yards. Needs a lot of room to be showy. Prune after flowering. Branches do not die back in winter.

### Orange-eye, Summer lilac
*B. davidi*

**Zone:** 5

**Height:** 15 feet

**Foliage and Flowers:** Half-inch flowers clustered on spikes up to 18 inches long. Foliage is an attractive silver-gray.

**Comments:** Full sun. Well-drained soil. Hardy. Open and shaggy in appearance. Plants die back to the ground each winter in cold climates.

## CINQUEFOIL, SHRUBBY
*Potentilla fruticosa*

**Zone:** 2

**Height:** 4 feet

**Foliage and Flowers:** Half- to 1-inch yellow or white single flowers appear from midsummer until fall.

**Comments:** Full sun. Well-drained soil. Hardy and pest resistant. Low growing and dense. Valued for its long periods of bloom. Use in foundation plantings or in low borders. Requires little pruning.

## COTONEASTER
*Cotoneaster sp.*

### Cranberry
*C. apiculatus*

**Zone:** 5

**Height:** 4 feet

**Foliage and Flowers:** Very small red-violet flowers in the spring, followed by ½-inch orange-red berries. Shiny green leaves.

**Comments:** Full sun or partial shade. Well-drained soil. Spreading, horizontal branching habit. Use on slopes or in foundation plantings. Can be trained on walls.

### Many-flowered
*C. multiflorus*

**Zone:** 6

**Height:** 12 feet

**Foliage and Flowers:** Half- to 1-inch white flowers cover the branches in spring, followed by large red berries in fall.

**Comments:** Full sun or partial shade. Well-drained soil. Very showy in all seasons. Use as a specimen plant.

## DAPHNE
*Deaphne sp..*

### February
*D. mezereum*

**Zone:** 5

**Height:** 4–5 feet

**Foliage and Flowers:** Small, pinkish, very fragrant flowers in clusters along the stems in early spring, followed by ½-inch red poisonous berries.

**Comments:** Full sun or partial shade. Does best in light, sandy soil. Small and upright in growth habit. Needs some winter protection in cold areas. Keep roots cool in warm weather by mulching. Use as a specimen plant.

## DEUTZIA
*Deutzia sp.*

### Fuzzy
*D. scabra*

**Zone:** 6

**Height:** 7 feet

**Foliage and Flowers:** Single or double white or pink flowers completely cover the branches in early spring. Light green foliage. Several varieties with different shades of blooms are available.

**Comments:** Full sun or partial shade. Tolerant of most soil types. Plants very showy. Use as a specimen plant. Prune old wood each year; prune new wood after flowering.

## DOGWOOD
*Cornus sp.*

### Japanese
*C. kousa*

**Zone:** 6

**Height:** 20 feet

**Foliage and Flowers:** One- to 2-inch clusters of white flowers in late spring, gradually turning pinkish, followed by reddish, raspberrylike fruits. Leaves turn red in the fall.

**Comments:** Full sun or partial shade. Tolerant of most soil types. Use as a specimen plant. Very showy. Berries relished by birds.

### Red-osier
*C. sericea*

**Zone:** 2

**Height:** 7–10 feet

**Foliage and Flowers:** White flowers in 2½- to 3-inch loose clusters intermittently from late spring to midsummer, followed by clusters of inedible white berries. Leaves turn red in fall. Twigs are brilliant red in winter.

**Comments:** Full sun or partial shade. Tolerant of most soil types. Vigorous and hardy. Prefers moist areas. Reproduces by underground stolons, so plant in an area where space is not limited. Use in hedges, in screens, or on moist embankments near ponds. Berries are relished by birds.

## ELAEAGNUS
*Elaeagnus sp.*

### Autumn olive
*E. umbellata*

**Zone:** 2

**Height:** 18 feet

**Foliage and Flowers:** Tiny yellowish white, fragrant flowers appear in the spring, followed by scaly, brown, inedible berries that turn red in the fall. Leaves are dark green above and silvery below.

**Comments:** Full sun. Well-drained soil. Hardy. Use as hedges and screens. Requires little care.

### Cherry
*E. multiflora*

**Zone:** 5

**Height:** 6 feet

**Foliage and Flowers:** Three-quarter-inch fragrant flowers appear in late spring, followed by ½- to 1-inch red cherrylike berries. Foliage is dark green above, silvery beneath.

**Comments:** Full sun. Well-drained soil. Vigorous and hardy. Use as hedge and screen. Requires little care. Berries are edible and relished by birds. Soot resistant.

## ELDERBERRY

### American, Sweet
*Sambucus canadensis*

**Zone:** 4

**Height:** 8 feet

**Foliage and Flowers:** Eight- to 12-inch clusters of tiny white flowers appear in midsummer, followed by edible blue-black or red berries.

**Comments:** Full sun or partial shade. Rich, moist, well-drained soil. Large, vigorous, spreading plant. Use berries in wines and preserves. Fruit is relished by birds. Does best in wet area. Use in out-of-the-way places. Easily pruned.

## EUONYMUS
*Euonymus sp.*

### Winged
*E. alata*

**Zone:** 4

**Height:** 8 feet

**Foliage and Flowers:** Subtle flowers in spring, followed by pinkish red seed capsules in fall. Twigs lined with unusual bark ridges. 'Compacta,' a dwarf variety, reaches 4 feet tall.

**Comments:** Full sun or partial shade. Tolerant of most soil types. Very hardy and useful. Very showy throughout the year. Use as hedges, screens, or specimen plants. Little pruning required.

## FORSYTHIA
*Forsythia sp.*

### Arnold dwarf
*F. x intermedia 'Arnold Dwarf'*

**Zone:** 5

**Height:** 4 feet

**Foliage and Flowers:** Small greenish yellow flowers appear randomly over the plant in early spring. Foliage is deep green.

**Comments:** Full sun or partial shade. Tolerant of most soil types. Low growing with arching branches that root on contact with soil. Vigorous grower forms dense mat of foliage. Use as a ground cover on slopes and other areas where soil stabilization is important.

*Spring is never far behind when the spectacular golden-yellow flowers of forsythia burst into bloom.*

## Border
*F. x intermedia*

**Zone:** 5

**Height:** 10 feet

**Foliage and Flowers:** Two-inch, trumpetlike, yellow-gold flowers in early spring, followed by deep green foliage. Many varieties: 'Spring Glory,' 'Lynwood,' 'Primulina,' 'Spectabilis,' and 'Beatrix Farrand.'

**Comments:** Full sun or partial shade. Tolerant of most soil types. Vigorous and hardy. Graceful, arching branches. Give plenty of space for optimum beauty. Cut twigs in late winter for early indoor bloom. Prune after flowering.

## HIBISCUS

### Rose-of-sharon, shrub althaea
*Hibiscus syriacus*

**Zone:** 6

**Height:** 6–10 feet or more

**Foliage and Flowers:** Two- to 4-inch single, double, or semidouble flowers in late summer with light green foliage. Some varieties have variegated leaves. Flower colors include white, pink, red, blue, and violet bicolors.

**Comments:** Full sun or partial shade. Moist, well-drained soil. Soot resistant. Valued for its late-blooming color. Use in hard-to-plant, narrow areas. Plant as hedge, screen, or specimen plant. Hardy in seashore locations. Young plants need winter protection in cold climates. Can be trained to tree form through pruning.

# HONEYSUCKLE
*Lonicera sp.*

## Amur
*L. maacki*

**Zone:** 3

**Height:** 15 feet

**Foliage and Flowers:** Small, whitish yellow, very fragrant flowers in late spring, followed by ¼-inch scarlet, inedible berries held well into winter.

**Comments:** Full sun or partial shade. Well-drained soil. Cold resistant. Later flowering than other honeysuckle varieties. Upright and not as spreading in growth habit as other varieties. Berries are relished by birds. Plants stay attractive late in the season. Evergreen in warm climates. Use as hedges, screens, or specimen plants.

# HYDRANGEA
*Hydrangea sp.*

## Hills-of-snow
*H. arborescens 'grandiflora'*

**Zone:** 4

**Height:** 4 feet

**Foliage and Flowers:** Six-inch clusters of tiny white flowers in rounded heads cover plant in midsummer. Large bright green leaves.

**Comments:** Full sun or partial shade. Rich, moist, well-drained soil. Dense and globular in shape. Very showy in flower. Often dies back in cold winter areas. Use in foundation plantings or in low, informal hedges. Prune in early spring before new growth.

## Peegee
*H. paniculata 'grandiflora'*

**Zone:** 4

**Height:** 30 feet

**Foliage and Flowers:** Twelve-inch pyramidal clusters of flowers cover the plant in midsummer. Blossoms are white, gradually turning to pink or purple and cling well into winter.

**Comments:** Full sun or partial shade. Rich, moist, well-drained soil. Can be trained to tree form. Use as a specimen plant in large yards. Cut flower clusters for dried bouquets. Pruning will increase size by encouraging more vigorous growth.

## KERRIA
*Kerria japonica*

**Zone:** 5

**Height:** 8 feet

**Foliage and Flowers:** Two-inch yellow flowers bloom in mid-May. Popular for green twigs in winter.

**Comments:** Full sun or partial shade. Tolerant of most soil types but prefers well-drained. Use as shrub border or specimen. Prune after blooms fade. May suffer winterkill; cut dead wood in early spring.

## LILAC
*Syringa sp.*

### Common
*S. vulgaris*

**Zone:** 4

**Height:** 20 feet

**Foliage and Flowers:** Half-inch fragrant flowers in clusters 6 to 8 inches long. Flowers can be single or double, depending on variety. Colors include violet, blue, pink, white, yellow, and magenta. Foliage is glossy green. More than 400 varieties.

*Prune lilac bushes in early summer after the fragrant blossoms fade to encourage more blooming the following year*

**Comments:** Well-drained soil. Full sun. Dense, vigorous, upright growth. Use as specimen plants, hedges, or screens. Cold resistant. Cut off dying flowers and seed clusters to promote better growth. Prune old wood yearly during dormancy. Remove most young unwanted suckers.

### Hungarian
*S. josikaea*

**Zone:** 4

**Height:** 12 feet

**Foliage and Flowers:** Quarter-inch red-purple fragrant flowers on clusters 4 to 6 inches long in late spring. Foliage is shiny green.

**Comments:** Full sun. Well-drained soil. Valued for its late blooms. Cut off dying flowers and seed clusters to promote better growth. Use as a specimen plant in large yards or in screens and hedges. Prune old wood yearly during dormancy. Remove young unwanted suckers when they appear, but be sure to leave some to keep plants vigorous and to replace dead branches.

---

# MOCK ORANGE
*Philadelphus sp.*

### Lemoine
*P. x lemoinei*

**Zone:** 5

**Height:** 4–8 feet

**Foliage and Flowers:** One- to 2-inch single or double fragrant white flowers in early summer.

**Comments:** Full sun or partial shade. Moist, rich, well-drained soil. Use as a specimen plant or in shrub border. Needs little pruning, except of dead wood.

### Virginalis
*P. x virginalis*

**Zone:** 5

**Height:** 5–9 feet

**Foliage and Flowers:** One- to 2-inch single or double fragrant white flowers in early summer. Dwarf varieties grow to 3 feet.

**Comments:** Full sun or partial shade. Moist, rich, well-drained soil. Very showy with delicate flowers. Use as specimen plants or in shrub borders. Needs little pruning, except of dead wood.

---

# PEARLBUSH
*Exochorda sp.*

### Pearlbush
*E. racemosa*

**Zone:** 5

**Height:** 10–12 feet

**Foliage and Flowers:** Strings of white buds open into 2-inch single flowers in mid-spring.

**Comments:** Full sun. Tolerant of most soil types. Use as specimen plant in large yards. More hardy with fewer flowers than 'Wilson' pearlbush.

## PEONY, TREE
*Paeonia suffruticosa*

**Zone:** 5

**Height:** 7 feet

**Foliage and Flowers:** Six- to 12-inch single, semidouble, or double flowers appear in late spring. Many colors and varieties. Foliage is gray-green.

**Comments:** Partial shade; can tolerate full sun. Rich, moist, well-drained soil. Very showy with flashy flowers. Use as specimen plants or in beds. Protect in winter in cold climates. Hardier than it looks. Occasionally needs staking.

## PRIVET
*Ligustrum sp.*

### Border
*L. obtusifolium*

**Zone:** 4

**Height:** 9 feet

**Foliage and Flowers:** Quarter-inch white flowers in 1- to 3-inch clusters in early summer, followed by small black berries in the fall. Leathery green foliage. 'Regal' privet or 'Regelianum' grows to 4 feet.

**Comments:** Full sun or partial shade. Tolerant of most soil types. Quick growing and attractive. Very dense with horizontal branches. Use in clipped or unclipped hedges and screens or use as a specimen plant. Berries are relished by birds. Soot tolerant.

## PUSSY WILLOW
*Salix sp.*

### Goat willow, French
*S. caprea*

**Zone:** 5

**Height:** 25 feet

**Foliage and Flowers:** Twigs are covered with 1- to 2-inch silvery pink catkins in early spring that gradually turn yellow with pollen. Leaves are light gray-green.

**Comments:** Full sun. Moist, well-drained soil. Quick growing. Use in screens or as specimen plants. Prune after catkins disappear. Cut twigs in late winter for indoor bouquets.

### Pussy willow
*S. discolor*

**Zone:** 2

**Height:** 20 feet

**Foliage and Flowers:** Twigs are covered with 1-inch white catkins in early spring that gradually turn yellow with pollen. Foliage is gray-green.

**Comments:** Full sun. Moist, well-drained soil. Quick growing. Smaller, hardier, and blooms later than goat willow. Cut twigs in late winter for attractive seasonal indoor bouquets. Use in screens or as specimen plants. Prune after fuzzy catkins disappear.

## QUINCE
*Chaenomeles sp.*

### Flowering
*C. speciosa*

**Zone:** 5

**Height:** 6 feet

**Foliage and Flowers:** One- to 2-inch single or double flowers cluster on branches in mid-spring, followed by 1-inch yellow-green fruits. Pink, red, bicolors, and white flowers, depending on variety.

**Comments:** Full sun. Well-drained soil. Very showy. Use fruits in jellies and jams. Use as specimen plants, borders, and hedges.

## RHODODENDRON, AZALEA
*Rhododendron sp.*

### Albrecht
*R. albrechti*

**Zone:** 6

**Height:** 5 feet

**Foliage and Flowers:** Two-inch rose-colored blossoms cover plant in spring.

*The rhododendron species contains many varieties, most of which are large and flourish in partly shaded areas with acidic soil.*

45

# Directory of Shrubs

**Comments:** Full sun or partial shade. Moist, acid soil. Hardy and fragrant. (For other rhododendrons, see pages 56–57.)

## Mollis hybrid, Chinese
*R. molle*

**Zone:** 6

**Height:** 5 feet

**Foliage and Flowers:** Two- to 3-inch flowers in late spring: pink, yellow, salmon, and white.

**Comments:** Full sun or partial shade. Moist, acid soil. Vigorous showy hybrids. Use in beds, in foundation plantings, or as accent.

## SPIREA
*Spiraea sp.*

## Big Nippon
*S. nipponica 'rotundifolia'*

**Zone:** 5

**Height:** 5–8 feet

**Foliage and Flowers:** Tiny white flowers in flat clusters in late spring. Foliage is attractive blue-green.

**Comments:** Full sun or partial shade. Tolerant of most soil types. Use as specimen plants or in shrub borders. More upright in growth than other varieties. Prune after flowers fade.

## Bridal-wreath
*S. prunifolia*

**Zone:** 5

**Height:** 6 feet

**Foliage and Flowers:** Half-inch double white flowers line branches in mid-spring. Leaves turn red-orange in fall.

**Comments:** Full sun or partial shade. Tolerant of most soil types. A popular spirea. Showy. Long arching branches. Use as a specimen plant or in shrub borders. Prune after flowers fade.

## Bumalda
*S. x bumalda*

**Zone:** 6

**Height:** 2 feet

**Foliage and Flowers:** Tiny pink flowers in flat 4- to 6-inch clusters on spikes in midsummer and often blooming through fall. 'Froebeli' or

'Froebel,' a popular variety, grows slightly taller.

**Comments:** Full sun or partial shade. Tolerant of most soil types. Use in shrub borders, foundation plantings, or rock gardens. Prune in early spring while plants are dormant. If old flowers are kept trimmed, blooming period is often prolonged.

## SUMAC
*Rhus sp.*

### Shining, dwarf
*R. copallina*

**Zone:** 5

**Height:** 20 feet

**Foliage and Flowers:** Tiny greenish yellow flowers on 4- to 5-inch spikes, followed by red, hairy berrylike fruits. Foliage is lustrous green, scarlet in the fall.

**Comments:** Full sun. Tolerant of most soil types. Quick growing. Use as a specimen tree or as a backdrop in a shrub border. Attractive in fall. Pruning will encourage more stems to grow. Plant both sexes to get fruit.

## SYMPHORICARPOS
*Symphoricarpos sp.*

### Chenault coralberry
*S. x chenaulti*

**Zone:** 5

**Height:** 3 feet

**Foliage and Flowers:** Inconspicuous pink flowers in midsummer, followed by small red berries, white on one side in fall.

**Comments:** Full sun or partial shade. Tolerant of most soil types. Berries are attractive in fall. Use in shrub borders; use low forms as vigorous ground covers. Gracefully arching branches. Spreads by underground runners. Prune in early spring while dormant.

## VIBURNUM
*Viburnum sp.*

### Arrowwood
*V. dentatum*

**Zone:** 3

**Height:** 15 feet

**Foliage and Flowers:** Tiny white flowers in 1- to 3-inch clusters in early summer, followed by blue berries in fall. Red foliage in fall.

**Comments:** Full sun or partial shade. Well-drained soil. Use as a specimen plant or in shrub borders. Berries relished by birds. Little pruning needed.

## European cranberry bush
### V. opulus

**Zone:** 3

**Height:** 12 feet

**Foliage and Flowers:** Tiny white flowers in 2- to 4-inch clusters, surrounded by a margin of ½-inch blossoms in late spring, followed by red berries in fall. Foliage of all varieties turns red in fall. 'Nanum' variety grows to 2 feet; Compactum,' to 5 feet.

**Comments:** Full sun or partial shade. Well-drained soil. Dense and vigorous. Use tall forms in shrub borders or screens. Use low forms in edgings and rock gardens. Needs little pruning.

## Fragrant snowball
### V. x carlcephalum

**Zone:** 5

**Height:** 9 feet

**Foliage and Flowers:** Small white fragrant flowers in rounded 4- to 5-inch heads, followed by red berries turning black as they mature. Foliage turns red in fall.

**Comments:** Full sun or partial shade. Well-drained soil. Use as a specimen plant or in shrub borders. Berries relished by birds. Little pruning needed.

## Japanese snowball
### V. plicatum

**Zone:** 5

**Height:** 10 feet

**Foliage and Flowers:** Tiny white flowers in 2- to 4-inch rounded ball-like clusters in late spring. Leaves turn red in the fall. 'Tomentosum' variety has a ring of ½-inch blossoms surrounding each flower cluster.

**Comments:** Full sun or partial shade. Well-drained soil. Use as a specimen plant or in a shrub border. Hardier than European snowball. Needs little pruning.

## Sargent cranberry bush
### V. sargenti

**Zone:** 6

**Height:** 12 feet

**Foliage and Flowers:** Tiny white flowers in 2- to 3-inch clusters surrounded by a margin of ½-inch blossoms during mid-spring and followed by red berries. 'Flavum' variety has golden yellow berries.

**Comments:** Full sun or partial shade. Well-drained soil. Similar to European cranberry bush. Very vigorous and hardy. Use in shrub borders, as screens, or as specimen plants. Berries relished by birds. Needs little pruning.

# WEIGELA
*Weigela sp.*

### Old-fashioned
*W. florida*

**Zone:** 5

**Height:** 8–10 feet

**Foliage and Flowers:** One-inch pink trumpetlike flowers cover plant in late spring. Foliage is deep green. 'Variegata' variety has yellowish white leaf margins. 'Alba' variety has white flowers.

**Comments:** Full sun or partial shade. Tolerant of most soil types. Graceful, arching branches. Use as a specimen plant or border. Prune after flowers fade.

*Funnel-shaped flowers of the weigela bloom on arching branches from late spring to early summer.*

# WITCH HAZEL
*Hamamelis sp.*

### Chinese
*H. mollis*

**Zone:** 5

**Height:** 30 feet

**Foliage and Flowers:** One- to 2-inch unusual, yellow ribbonlike, fragrant flowers cover plant in early spring. Yellow foliage in fall.

**Comments:** Full sun or partial shade. Rich, moist, well-drained soil. Grown for early bloom and scent. Dense and rounded. Use as specimen plants or in shrub borders. Needs little pruning.

### Common
*H. virginiana*

**Zone:** 5

**Height:** 15 feet

**Foliage and Flowers:** Half- to 1-inch yellow ribbonlike flowers appear in late fall. Foliage turns yellow at the same time.

**Comments:** Full sun. Rich, moist, well-drained soil. Grown for late bloom. Use as shrub backdrop. Often open and loose in growth. Soot tolerant.

# BROAD-LEAVED EVERGREEN SHRUBS

## ANDROMEDA
*P.ieris sp.*

### Japanese, Lily-of-the-valley bush
*P. japonica*

**Zone:** 6

**Height:** 10 feet

**Foliage and Flowers:** Small white fragrant flowers in drooping 5-inch clusters of 3 to 5 in mid-spring. Foliage is bright green. Young foliage is bronze.

**Comments:** Full sun or partial shade. Well-drained, slightly acid soil. Showy, so makes a good ornamental shrub. Use in borders, foundation plantings, or as specimen plants. Needs some protection in cold climates. Prune after flowers fade.

## BARBERRY
*Berberis sp.*

### Black
*B. gagnepaini*

**Zone:** 6

**Height:** 6 feet

**Foliage and Flowers:** Small yellow flowers cover the plant in late spring, followed by blue-black berries in the fall. Glossy green leaves on stems armed with small, but sharp, thorns.

**Comments:** Full sun or partial shade. Moist, well-drained soil. Dense branching habit. Showy, in all seasons. Use as a hedge or a border. Needs little pruning.

# BOXWOOD
*Buxus sp.*

## Common box
*B. sempervirens*

**Zone:** 6

**Height:** 15 feet. Many shorter varieties.

**Foliage and Flowers:** Small glossy green leaves. 'Argenteo variegata' has leaves spotted with white.

**Comments:** Full sun or partial shade. Moist, well-drained soil. Many varieties. Use as specimen plants or borders. Needs winter protection in cold climates. Easily sheared but needs little pruning to look tidy.

# CAMELLIA
*Camellia sp.*

## Common
*C. japonica*

**Zone:** 8

**Height:** 45 feet

**Foliage and Flowers:** Three- to 6-inch single or double showy flowers appear in mid-fall and continue through spring. Colors include red, pink, white, and bicolors. Attractive glossy green leaves.

**Comments:** Partial shade. Moist, rich, well-drained, acid soil. Many varieties. Use as specimen plants or in shrub borders. Needs winter protection in cold winter areas. Needs little pruning.

# COTONEASTER
*Cotoneaster sp.*

## Rock
*C. horizontalis*

**Zone:** 6

**Height:** 3 feet

**Foliage and Flowers:** Small pink flowers appear in early summer, followed by bright red berries in early fall. Glossy green leaves. In cold climates, leaves turn orange in the fall and drop off. 'Variegata' variety has leaves edged with white.

**Comments:** Well-drained, slightly alkaline soil kept on the dry side. Full sun. Flat spreading branches. Use in rock gardens or on hard-to-plant slopes as a ground cover. Prune in early spring before new growth.

## DAPHNE
*Daphne sp.*

### Burkwood
*D. x burkwoodi*

**Zone:** 6

**Height:** 4 feet

**Foliage and Flowers:** Half-inch whitish fragrant flowers appear in mid-spring, followed by small red berries in midsummer. Leaves are gray-green. Often drops its leaves in early spring in cold climates.

**Comments:** Partial shade. Moist, well-drained soil. Dense, moundlike growth habit. Does not like wet soil. Often touchy about growing conditions. Use as specimen plants or in shrub borders. Poisonous if eaten. Needs little pruning.

## ELAEAGNUS, THORNY
*Elaeagnus pungens*

**Zone:** 7

**Height:** 15 feet

**Foliage and Flowers:** Small white fragrant flowers in mid-fall, followed by brown berries changing to red in the spring. Leaves are green above, silvery beneath. Variegated forms available. Twigs are thorny.

**Comments:** Full sun or partial shade. Tolerant of most soil types. Hardy, vigorous, and pest-free. Use in windbreaks, screens, or hedges. Easily sheared in early spring before new growth.

## EUONYMUS
*Euonumus sp.*

### Big leaf winter creeper
*E. fortunei 'Sarcoxie'*

**Zone:** 6

**Height:** 4 feet

**Foliage and Flowers:** Tiny inconspicuous flowers in the spring, followed by pinkish seed capsules that open to reveal orange berries inside.

**Comments:** Full sun or partial shade. Tolerant of most soil types. Will lose leaves in cold climates. This rambling shrub can be trained on walls or used as a ground cover. Use in foundation plantings and rock gardens. Easily pruned all year.

## Spreading
*E. kiautschovica*

**Zone:** 7

**Height:** 10 feet

**Foliage and Flowers:** Tiny inconspicuous flowers in the spring, followed by pinkish seed capsules in the fall. The capsules open to reveal orange berries inside. Foliage is light glossy green.

**Comments:** Full sun or partial shade. Tolerant of most soil types. Hardier than japonica species in cold climates. Use in foundation plantings, in shrub borders, and as specimen plants. Easily sheared any time of year.

## FIRE THORN
*Pyracantha sp.*

### Scarlet
*P. coccinea*

**Zone:** 7

**Height:** 6 feet

**Foliage and Flowers:** Small white clusters of flowers appear in the spring, followed by bright scarlet berries in the fall and winter. Twigs are thorny. Varieties 'Kasan' and 'Pauciflora' have orange-red berries.

**Comments:** Full sun. Tolerant of most soil types if kept on the dry side. Colorful. Berries are relished by birds. Use in borders, as espalier on a wall, or as specimen plants. Loses some leaves in cold climates. Easily sheared any time.

## HEATH
*Erica sp.*

### Cross-leaved
*E. tetralix*

**Zone:** 4

**Height:** 2 feet

**Foliage and Flowers:** Small rose-colored flowers in 1- to 3-inch clusters appear in midsummer. Leaves are hairy, gray, and needlelike.

**Comments:** Full sun. Moist, well-drained, acid soil. Use in beds, borders, or rock gardens. More cold hardy than other varieties. Mulch for best results. Prune in early spring.

# Directory of Shrubs

## HEATHER
*Calluna vulgaris*

**Zone:** 5

**Height:** 3 feet

**Foliage and Flowers:** Small single or double flowers appear in midsummer in 1- to 4-inch clusters. Many varieties. Flower colors include rose, purple, pink, white, and coral. Foliage is green or yellow, bronze in the fall.

**Comments:** Full sun. Tolerant of most soil types; prefers slightly acid soil. Use in beds, in foundation plantings, in rock gardens, or as a ground cover. Mulch for best results. Prune in early spring before new growth begins.

## HOLLY
*Ilex sp.*

### Chinese
*I. cornuta*

**Zone:** 7

**Height:** 9 feet

**Foliage and Flowers:** Tiny inconspicuous flowers in early summer, followed by bright red berries in the fall and winter. Leaves are glossy green with pointed tips. 'D'or' variety has yellow berries.

**Comments:** Full sun or partial shade. Well-drained, slightly acid soil. Female plant can produce fruit without aid of pollen. Needs protection from severe weather in cold climates. Needs little pruning; best done in early spring.

## LAUREL

### Mountain, Calico bush
*Kalmia latifolia*

**Zone:** 5

**Height:** 10 feet

**Foliage and Flowers:** One-inch cuplike flowers appear in 3- to 6-inch clusters in early summer. Leaves are glossy green. Colors include white, pink, and rose. 'Fuscata' variety has a purple band on the inside of each flower.

**Comments:** Partial shade. Moist, acid soil. Very hardy and cold resistant. Use in shrub borders or in mass plantings for effect. Needs little pruning, but it is best done after flowers fade. Clip off developing seed capsules for more vigorous growth.

# LEUCOTHOE, DROOPING
*Leucothoe fontanesiana*

**Zone:** 5

**Height:** 6 feet

**Foliage and Flowers:** Small white, lily-of-the-valley-type clusters appear along the stems in early summer. Leaves are glossy green and turn bronze in the fall.

**Comments:** Partial or deep shade. Moist, well-drained, acid soil. Use in shrub borders and foundation plantings. Cut off old canes every spring to keep plants vigorous. Leaves drop off in cold climates.

# OLEANDER
*Nerium oleander*

**Zone:** 8

**Height:** 20 feet

**Foliage and Flowers:** Two- to 3-inch single or double fragrant flowers in early spring continue to bloom throughout the summer. Colors are red, yellow, white, rose, and pink. Foliage is narrow and glossy green.

**Comments:** Full sun. Rich, moist, well-drained soil. Tolerant of hot, dry conditions. Soot resistant. All parts of the plant are poisonous. Can be trained to tree form. Use in tubs, shrub borders, or screens, or as specimen plants.

# PHOTINIA
*Photina serrulata*

**Zone:** 7

**Height:** 40 feet

**Foliage and Flowers:** Small white flowers in clusters 4 to 7 inches wide appear in mid-spring, followed by red berries in the winter. Foliage is bronze when young, later turning glossy green.

**Comments:** Full sun or partial shade. Well-drained soil. Very vigorous and hardy. Keep dry during the summer. Use in shrub borders, in screens, or as specimen plants. Must be pruned occasionally to prevent legginess.

# Directory of Shrubs

## PITTOSPORUM, JAPANESE
*Pittosporum tobira*

**Zone:** 8

**Height:** 18 feet

**Foliage and Flowers:** Small white fragrant flowers appear in mid-spring. Leaves are leathery and green. 'Variegata' has leaves variegated with white.

**Comments:** Full sun or partial shade. Tolerant of most soil types. Very hardy and pest resistant. Use in screens, hedges, and shrub borders. Prune after new growth begins and again later in the season.

## PRIVET
*Ligustrum sp.*

### Glossy
*L. lucidum*

**Zone:** 8

**Height:** 30 feet

**Foliage and Flowers:** Small white flowers in 4- to 8-inch clusters appear in late summer, followed by blue-black berries. 'Tricolor' variety has pale yellow leaf margins that have a pinkish hue when young.

**Comments:** Full sun or partial shade. Tolerant of most soil types. Very hardy and pest resistant. Use in screens, hedges, and shrub borders. Prune after new growth begins and again later in the season.

## RHODODENDRON, AZALEAS
*Rhododendron sp.*

### Glen Dale
*R. 'Glenn Dale Hybrid'*

**Zone:** 7

**Height:** 5 feet

**Foliage and Flowers:** One- to 3-inch single or double flowers cover the plant in spring. Foliage is glossy green. Many colors. More than 400 varieties.

**Comments:** Partial shade. Well-drained, acid soil. Dense and spreading. Use in beds, foundation plantings, or shrub borders, or in mass plantings for display. Cut off fading flowers for more vigorous flowering the next year. Keep mulched for best results.

## RHODODENDRON, RHODODENDRON
*Rhododendron sp.*

### Carolina
*R. carolinianum*

**Zone:** 6

**Height:** 6 feet

**Foliage and Flowers:** Three-inch clusters of rose-violet flowers cover the plant in mid-spring. Leaves are glossy green above with brown undersides. 'Album' variety has white flowers.

**Comments:** Full sun or partial shade. Rich, moist, well-drained, acid soil. Dense and moundlike. Earlier to bloom than other varieties. Use in beds, foundation plantings, or shrub borders, or in mass plantings for display. Cut off fading flowers for more vigorous flowering the next year. May need winter protection in some areas. Leaf edges curl under when cold. Keep mulched for best results.

(For other rhododendrons, see page 45).

## ROSEMARY
*Rosemarinus officinalis*

**Zone:** 7

**Height:** 4 feet

**Foliage and Flowers:** Half- to 1-inch fragrant violet flowers cover the plant in late winter and early spring. Leaves are glossy green with a pleasant aroma. 'Prostratus,' a trailing variety, averages 6 inches in height.

**Comments:** Full sun. Tolerant of most soil types. Use in beds, shrub borders, and hedges. Needs little pruning. Keep on the dry side to prevent rapid, spindly growth.

## VIBURNUM
*Viburnum sp.*

### Laurustinus
*V. tinus*

**Zone:** 7

**Height:** 10 feet

**Foliage and Flowers:** Small pinkish flowers appear in late winter, followed by shiny blue berries in midsummer, gradually turning black. Leaves are glossy green.

**Comments:** Partial shade. Well-drained soil, kept dry. Use in hedges and screens. Berries are relished by birds. Keep plants dry after midsummer to harden new growth. Prune in early spring before new growth.

## NARROW-LEAVED EVERGREEN (CONIFEROUS) SHRUBS

*A popular choice for privacy screens, the arborvitae are compact, stand-up classics that require very little care.*

## ARBORVITAE, AMERICAN
*Thuja occidentalis*

**Zone:** 3

**Height:** Varieties vary; average 7–10 feet

**Shape and Foliage:** Most are compact pyramidals. Green or blue-green, odd scalelike foliage in fan formation.

**Comments:** Rich, moist, well-drained soil. Slow growing. Use as foundation plants or in hedges. Cannot tolerate heat. Prune in early spring before new growth.

## CEPHALOTAXUS
### Japanese plum yew
*Cephalotaxus harringtonia*

**Zone:** 6

**Height:** 30 feet

**Shape and Foliage:** Multistemmed; wide spreading. 'Fastigiata' cultivar is columnar in habit. Dark green with 1½ -inch needles.

**Comments:** Moist, well-drained, acid soil. Similar to yews but not as dense. Use in hedge or screen. Bears 1-inch, plum-shape purple-green fruits. Shear in spring before new growth.

## CRYPTOMERIA
### Japanese cedar
*Cryptomeria japonica 'nana'*

**Zone:** 5

**Height**: 3 feet

**Shape and Foliage:** Dwarf variety. Broad, mound shaped. Dark green, needlelike foliage.

**Comments:** Moist, well-drained soil. Use in foundation plantings. Handsome in patio tubs.

## FALSE CYPRESS
*Chamaecyparis sp.*

### Dwarf hinoki
*C. obtusa 'nana aurea'*

**Zone:** 5

**Height:** 4 feet

**Shape and Foliage:** Broad, flattened foliage; scalelike and fan-shaped.

**Comments:** Moist, well-drained, slightly acid soil. Slow growing. Use in rock gardens or around foundations. Prune any time.

### Plume
*C. pisifera 'plumosa'*

**Zone:** 4

**Height:** Variable with shearing. Up to 100 feet

**Shape and Foliage:** Dense foliage; fluffy, scalelike, and feathery green. Also a gold variety.

**Comments:** Moist, well-drained, slightly acid soil. Slow growing. Use as a specimen tree. Often unsightly when mature. Prune any time.

## JUNIPER
*Juniperus sp.*

### Dwarf common
*J. communis 'compressa'*

**Zone:** 3

**Height**: 4 feet

**Shape and Foliage:** Broadly spreading. Foliage is grayish green with ¼-inch needles.

**Comments:** Well-drained soil. Good foundation plant. Prune any time. Plant in rock gardens.

# Directory of Shrubs

## Hollywood
*J. chinensis 'torulosa'*

**Zone:** 4

**Height:** 20 feet

**Shape and Foliage:** Broadly conical. Tufted needles and scales.

**Comments:** Well-drained soil. Use as a specimen tree. Interesting, twisted branching habit. Do not prune. Also a variegated form.

## Pfitzer
*J. chinensis 'pfitzerana'*

**Zone:** 4

**Height:** 6 feet

**Shape and Foliage:** Dense; broad, flat-topped. Feathery, scalelike foliage and needles.

**Comments:** Well-drained soil. Fast growing. Tolerant of partial shade. Needs constant pruning. An excellent foundation plant to go with other plants.

## Shore
*J. conferta*

**Zone:** 6

**Height:** 1 foot

**Shape and Foliage:** Dense; low spreading. Quarter-inch green needles.

**Comments:** Prefers sandy seashore locations. Use as a ground cover in sandy, hard-to-plant areas. Prune any time.

# PINE
*Pinus Sp.*

## Bristle-cone, Hickory
*P. aristata*

**Zone:** 6

**Height:** 10–40 feet

**Shape and Foliage:** Variable shape. Dark blue-green needles in clusters of five, 1 to 1¾ inches long.

**Comments:** Well-drained soil. Slow growing. Picturesque branching habit. Use as a specimen tree or as an accent. Good in patio tubs, so it can be moved for effect. Prune after spring growth has started.

# SPRUCE

## Dwarf white
*Picea glauca 'conica'*

**Zone:** 5

**Height:** 8 feet

**Shape and Foliage:** Dense; pyramidal. Single trunk. Half-inch tufted, light green needles.

**Comments:** Well-drained soil. Slow growing. Use in conjunction with low- growing shrubs, or plant as a specimen tree. Needs no pruning.

# YEW
*Taxus sp.*

## Irish
*T. baccata 'fastigiata'*

**Zone:** 7

**Height:** 15 feet

**Shape and Foliage:** Dense; narrow columnar or rounded. Lustrous dark green, 1-inch needles. Also a golden variety.

**Comments:** Well-drained, slightly alkaline soil. Upright picturesque branching. Use in hedges or screens. Fleshy red berries in fall. Prune after spring growth has begun.

## Spreading English
*T. baccata 'repandens'*

**Zone:** 6

**Height:** 3 feet

**Shape and Foliage:** Dense, low spreading, flat. Lustrous green 1-inch needles.

**Comments:** Well-drained, slightly alkaline soil. Branches slightly pendulous. Use in foundation plantings or as a ground cover. Bears fall fruit.

# Zone Map

**Consider Your Climate** The key to successful gardening is knowing what plants are best suited to your area and when to plant them. This is true for every type of gardening. Climate maps, such as the one opposite, give a good idea of the extremes in temperature by zones. The zone-number listings tell you the coldest temperature a plant typically can edure.

By choosing plants best adapted to the different zones, and by planting them at the right time, you will have many more successes.

The climate in your area is a mixture of many different weather patterns: sun, snow, rain, wind, and humidity. To be a good gardener, you should know, on an average, how cold the garden gets in winter, how much rainfall it receives each year, and how hot or dry it becomes in a typical summer. You can obtain this general information from your state agricultural school or your county extension agent. In addition, acquaint yourself with the mini-climates in your neighborhood, based on such factors as wind protection gained from a nearby hill, or humidity and cooling offered by a local lake or river. Then carry the research further by studying the microclimates that characterize your own plot of ground.

**Here are a few points to keep in mind:**

- Plants react to exposure. Southern and western exposures are sunnier and warmer than northern or eastern ones. Light conditions vary greatly even in a small yard. Match your plants' needs to the correct exposure.
- Wind can damage many plants, by either drying the soil or knocking over fragile growth. Protect plants from both summer and winter winds to increase their odds of survival and to save yourself the time and energy of staking plants and watering more frequently.
- Consider elevation, too, when selecting plants. Cold air sweeps down hills and rests in low areas. These frost pockets are fine for some plantings, deadly for others. Plant vegetation that prefers a warmer environment on the tops or sides of hills, never at the bottom.
- Use fences, the sides of buildings, shrubs, and trees to your advantage. Watch the play of shadows, the sweep of winds, and the flow of snowdrifts in winter. These varying situations are ideal for some plants, harmful to others. In short, always look for ways to make the most of everything your yard has to offer.

# THE USDA PLANT HARDINESS MAP
## OF THE UNITED STATES AND CANADA

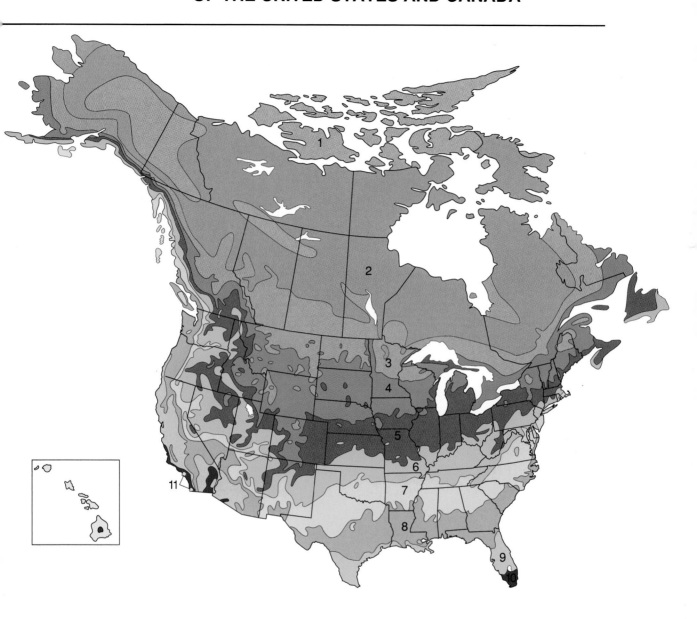

**RANGE OF AVERAGE ANNUAL MINIMUM
TEMPERATURES FOR EACH ZONE**

| | | |
|---|---|---|
| ZONE 1 | BELOW -50° F | |
| ZONE 2 | -50° TO -40° | |
| ZONE 3 | -40° TO -30° | |
| ZONE 4 | -30° TO -20° | |
| ZONE 5 | -20° TO -10° | |
| ZONE 6 | -10° TO 0° | |
| ZONE 7 | 0° TO 10° | |
| ZONE 8 | 10° TO 20° | |
| ZONE 9 | 20° TO 30° | |
| ZONE 10 | 30° TO 40° | |
| ZONE 11 | ABOVE 40° | |

# Index